DIVERSION
for Alto Saxophone and Concert Band
Piano Reduction by the Composer

Bernhard Heiden (1943)
edited by R. Mark Rogers

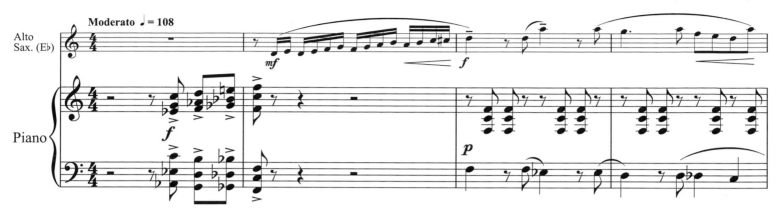

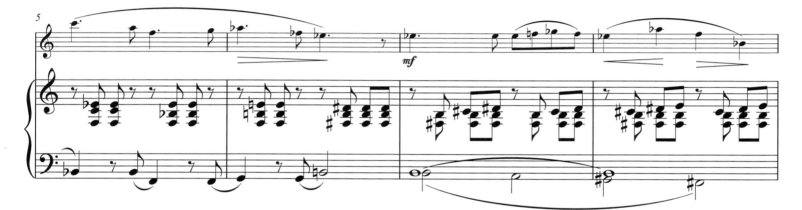

2

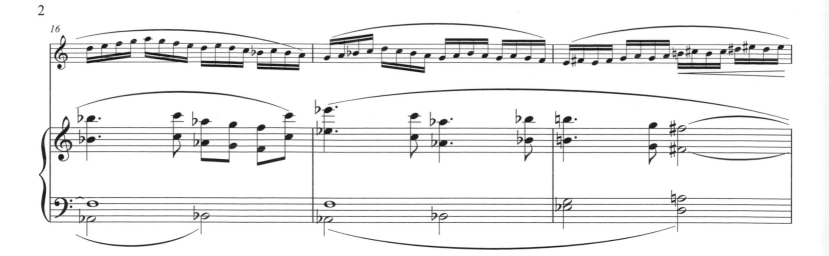

31 **Poco meno mosso**

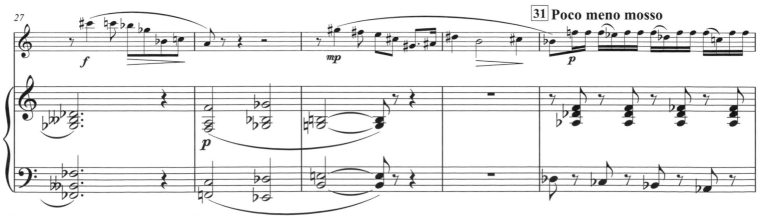

47 **Poco più mosso**

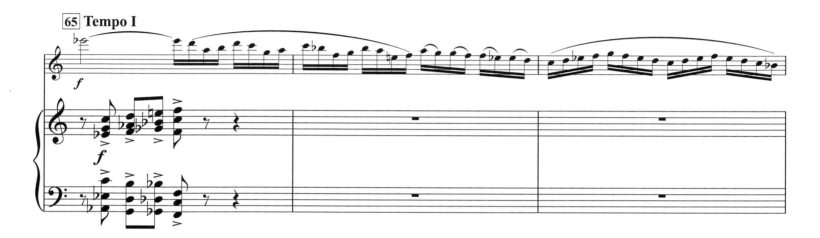

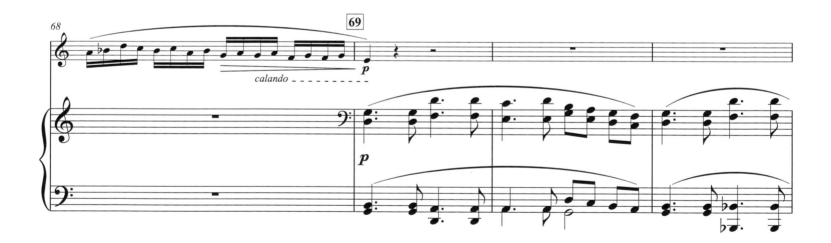

6

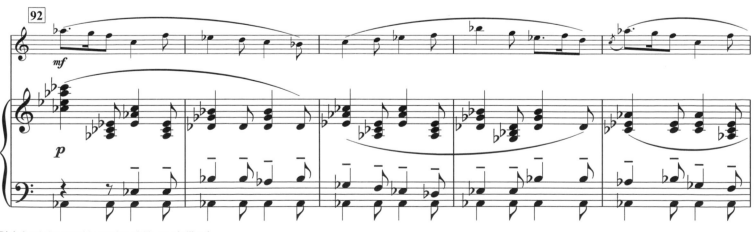

Solo Alto Saxophone (E♭)

DIVERSION
for Alto Saxophone and Concert Band

Bernhard Heiden (1943)
edited by R. Mark Rogers

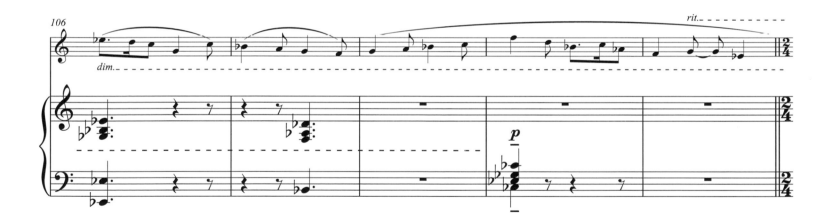

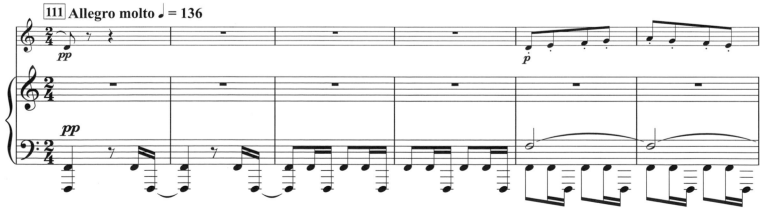

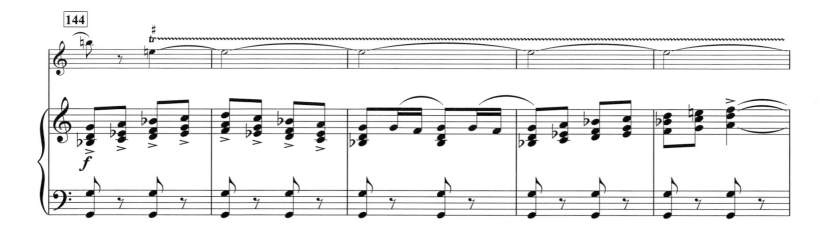

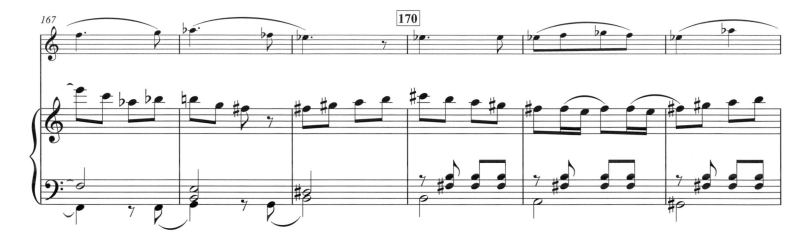

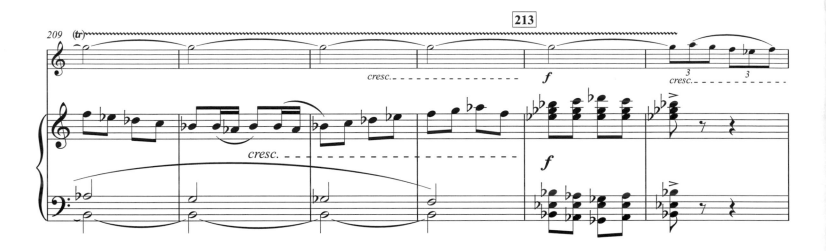